everyone
has
sher
favorite
(his or hers)
        by dick higgins
                (models from 7 of the 70's)
        by dick higgins
(his or hers)
favorite
sher
has
everyone

                                   1977
                        unpublished editions
       new york, new york, and barton, vermont
                        unpublished editions
                                   1977

LIBRARY OF CONGRESS CATALOGING IN PUBLICATION DATA

Higgins, Richard Carter.
  Everyone has sher favorite (his or hers).
  Poems.
  I. Title.
PS3558.I36E85   811'.5'4   77-4813
ISBN 0-914162-17-9
ISBN 0-914162-16-0 pbk.

copyright © 1971, 1976 and 1977 by richard c. higgins. all rights reserved. no portion of this text may be reproduced in any form whatever without permission in writing from the author or his duly authorized agent, except for brief passages quoted in a review written for a newspaper or a magazine, or a radio or television broadcast.

                manufactured in the united states of america.

some of the texts in this book first appeared in *Ausgabe, Da Vinci, Dramatika, Ear, The Barton Chronicle, Intermedia, Mouth of the Dragon, Poetry Australia, Poetry Mailing List, The Smith* and *Truck*. many thanks are due to the editors of those publications.

everyone has sher favorite (his or hers)

"true poetry is at the same time music and philosophy."
—giordano bruno (1591)

for ms. alison, first and last

Table of Contents

red dog, page 3

waiting for a friend, page 6

modern times, page 8

Symphony No. 1007, page 9

gilles, page 10

a comedy, page 11

the ear-batter, page 12

cent mots des cloches à noix, page 13

milwaukee poem, page 14

two things about the woods, page 15

a dance for maureen conner, page 16

(untitled) "vain man," page 17

the sixties, a pastiche, page 18

ducks tails shaking, page 23

hymn, page 24

Constellation No. 11, page 25

jolie julie, page 26

the nature of fish, page 27

Six Imitations for Piano and Pianist, page 28

Martin, page 29

for kathy k———, page 36

selling futures on art works, page 37

friend, what's going on here?, page 38

poem from or for bern porter, page 39

waltz macabre, page 40

Life, page 41

words are mirrors, page 42

conceptual forks, page 43

a commentary by the poet on "conceptual forks," page 44

definition, page 46

it could be you too, page 47

(untitled) "A HA," page 50

moving, page 51

fight, page 56

28 things to think about, a manifesto, page 57

song: "is round six," page 58

portrait of a woman, page 59

leather jacket vaudeville, page 60

to my brother and sister english teachers, page 61

old man, page 62

memories of the 1950's, page 63

to whom it may concern, page 64

deep summer together poem, page 65

Something Borrowed, page 71

Sonnet: "Of Barton winds my breath is made," page 72

abstand zum abstand veb, page 73

this word, page 75

3 reflections on poststructuralism, page 76

lyronic: no birding permitted, page 77

love song for straights, page 78

Put Differently, Another Socratic Question for
       Mike Belt, page 79

You're in the News Today, page 80

two insincerities, page 81

Appearances and Disappearance, page 84

everyone has sher favorite (his or hers)

red dog
(to be read aloud and spatialized)

    yellow flamingo
    blue dog
    red dog
    black dress

    black skull

    red bear
    blue dog
    red sex

    black lizard
    purple
    green flamingo
    black fish
    red bear
    red fish
    red turtle
    purple
    yellow fish
    red flamingo
    black dog
    blue lizard
    blue lizard
    purple dog
    yellow dog
    blue lizard
    blue turtle
    black dress

blue dress
purple dog
yellow
black dog
black turtle
yellow
purple turtle
purple bear
black
purple dog
blue house

yellow scales

green
yellow house

yellow turtle
red
black scales

purple turtle
green
yellow fish
yellow flamingo
blue
purple bear
black fish
blue turtle
green flamingo
black flamingo
black turtle
yellow dog
yellow flamingo

black fish
yellow fish
yellow flamingo
purple dog
green sex

black dog
yellow
blue turtle
black turtle
yellow flamingo
blue bear
red dog
yellow bear
black
black house

black lizard
green bear
green dress

black
green flamingo
yellow fish
red bear
blue
red turtle
purple dog
green flamingo
red

barton, vermont
4 august 1976

waiting for a friend

                    i
            delights
this snow delights
            delights me
                    me
            delights
this snow
            delights
                    me
                        delights
                    me
            delights
this snow
            delights
                    me
            delights me
this snow delights
            delights

ii

ah but then
   but
ah
   but
ah   so
         so do so
               so many things
                  many
                         things
                         things
                         things
                  many
               so many things
         so do so
ah   so
   but
ah
   but
ah but then

                                      milwaukee
                                  4 february, 1977

modern times

the secretariat bans the old men in the park and harasses the
 long hairs but helps the newly employed

the newly employed take care of the old men in the park

the long hairs feed the motorcycle girls what they need

the motorcycle girls assist the nurses and the eaters of wind
 pudding but they only nod to members of the secretariat

the nurses measure the eaters of wind pudding and these
 sometimes join the secretariat

the dice-hole drillers have nothing to do with the eaters of
 wind pudding but they often beat up the leatherjackets

the nurses usually help the dice-hole drillers

the leatherjackets often date members of the secretariat

what is the real relationship between the secretariat and the
 nurses?

berlin-wannsee
20. march '75

Symphony No. 1007

Place the grid over anything.
Perform the result.

> West Glover, Vermont
> May 21, 1977

gilles

    man in white, tall white stovepipe hat
    red ribbon, thirty yards, one end fastened to top of hat
    man turns around slowly (revolving stagelet?), winding
ribbon slowly and evenly down over him
        barber pole? candy cane?
        alaha ismarladik!

new york
february 22, 1976

a comedy

read this as a tragedy

                                        denver
                                        4.v.77

the ear-batter

bats
ears

barton, vermont
december 2, 1972

cent mots des cloches à noix

elle venut. je partit. je promenut. je vut. elle chantut. elle crachut. je venut. elle courrat. elle parlat. je montat. je fleurut.
je marchat. elle courrat. je rirat. elle pleurat. elle jouat. je reveillat. elle groignat. je chantat. elle sursautat. je criat. elle glapit. j'aboyat. elle grondat.
je circulat. elle posat. elle tournat. elle ronronnat. elle cuillat. je mourat. elle lavat. je complaignat. je marchat. elle promenat. je courrut. je promenat.
elle rirat. je sécouat. elle frappat. je ioulat. elle plaindrat. je bût. elle chevauchat. je franchit. elle golfat. je noyat. elle étranglat.
elle partit. je partit.

pour le jackson de vermont
le 12me août, 1970, et
retouffé en français le 10me
décember, 1973

milwaukee poem

a birth, a death,
a death, a birth.

rrrrring (4:30 AM)!— the sack just burst.
rrrrring (7:30 AM)!— she's born, and i'm *walking*
    to the hospital.

a birth.
a death.

hymn to the policeman's stretcher—
she'd have been 100 her next birthday.
she'd have her next 100 birthday been.
next she'd have 100 her birthday been.

a death.
a birth.

rrrrring— we do not have your number.
rrrrring— do not we have your number.

death death.
death birth.
birth death.
birth birth.

                              milwaukee
                              27 march, 1977

two things about the woods

one thing about the woods:
                              coming out of em
one more thing about the woods:
                              coming back to em

                              west glover, vermont
                              september 15th, 1974

a dance for maureen conner

i

a dance of the seven veils
but one that does not reveal
but which hides

naked
dancing into your shadows
concealed
at the end— darkness

ii

(a vocal dance, possibly to go with it):
the same but for voice
naturally nude
then slowly obscured by overlays

naturally nude
then artificial expressions
affected language
hysterical tone
forced and tight throat
constricted into screeches and scrawtches
finally constricted into silence

new york city
april 29, 1976

(untitled)

vain man
i feel your urge to come

      earth
it's time earth rest
it's time   rest

milwaukee
4 february, 1977

the sixties, a pastiche

music very bright
acid very bright
grass very bright
grass that's right
east seventh street very bright
east seventh street by night
east seventh street that's right
mod clothes outta sight
east seventh street by night
acid that's right
pop things by night
pop things in dim light
east seventh street very bright
music by night
east seventh street by night
pop things very bright
music with all our might

near the love in
after the discotheque
at the happening
in the head shop
by the discotheque
before the love in
at the student strike
after the head shop
by the student strike
by the student strike
before the peace march

now things and
love beads and

incense and
now things and
love beads and
love beads and
peacock feathers and
love beads and
smoke and
incense and
incense and
peacock feathers and
now things and
incense and
the beatles and

reginald and
barbro and
reginald and
reginald and
john and
me and
me and
carollee and
carollee and
carollee and
barbro and
john and
john and
carol and

   music by night
   acid outta sight
   east seventh street by night
   east seventh street outta sight
   grass with all our might
   pop things outta sight

east seventh street in dim light
pop things outta sight
grass with all our might
east seventh street very bright
music very bright
acid very bright
east seventh street very bright
music by night
grass very bright
grass with all our might
east seventh street by night

on a bus
tenderly
down empty blocks
on a bus
on a bus
tenderly
down empty blocks
tenderly
dimly
in the clouds
on a bus
in the clouds
down empty blocks
down empty blocks
tenderly
in the clouds
never never

by the love in
in the head shop
before the peace march
at the discotheque
after the discotheque

near the happening
before the love in
at the head shop
in the student strike

love beads and
incense and
the beatles and
love beads and
now things and
love beads and
smoke and
the beatles and
incense and
now things and
the beatles and
peacock feathers and

down empty blocks
in the clouds
in the clouds
dimly
down empty blocks
never never
dimly
in the clouds
down empty blocks
never never
never never
on a bus
in the clouds
down empty blocks
in the clouds
dimly
on a bus

dimly
down empty blocks
on a bus
in the clouds
dimly
on a bus
down empty blocks
tenderly

peacock feathers and
the beatles and
incense and
love beads and
smoke and
incense and
now things and

dancing
dancing
dancing
dancing (tatata)
(tatata)
dancing (tatata)
dancing
dancing (tatata)
(tatata)

                                      new york
                                      december 8, 1975

ducks tails shaking

rhetoric and dialectic
through both to the thing
or through one and the other

spanish peter separated them
agricola locates them
ramus merges them

the tree of life
blowing in the wind

a card, an idea, a phrase,

                                              new york
                                              3 january, 1977

hymn

lion church
church lion

sometimes a pebble
wanting to be an avalanche

lionly church
churchly lion

sometimes the immensity
of the still & small

lion
church
       church
           lion
       church
church
lion

                milwaukee
                13 february, 1977

Constellation No. 11

1) Choosing a word.

2) Choosing a length of time.

3) Starting to count out the length of time.

4) Silently.

5) Saying the word at the end of the length of time.

6) Lots of people doing this together.

Barton, Vermont
September 7, 1972

jolie julie

jolie julie est ma mimou

the sixth march of '77
milwaukee

the nature of fish

water water water water water water water water
   water water water water water water water
water water water water water water water water

   brothers   our
my   and   in   common
        sisters   life
                      among
                          hard
                              stones
                                and
                                  doubts
                                  &
water water water water water
water water water water water water water water water water
water water water water water water water water water water
   water water water water water

                                milwaukee
                                2 february, '77

Six Imitations for Piano and Pianist

Imitate:

    1. Bells all over the mountain,

    2. Ducks fighting,

    3. Geometry,

    4. The small intestine,

    5. Chords— not quite real chords,—

    6. Frogs and pianos in love.

Milwaukee
9 March, 1977

Martin

portrait of a sentimentalist

i

If you call me Martin, you won't be far from the truth.
I am here, I am alive.
To you it will seem as if I don't feel things. But I do, I do— I assure you.
All this is about me.
I *feel*, I *feel*— I *must* feel.
I pity the people who don't.
I don't care if it's pain, pleasure, numbness— I must feel it. I don't like to feel incomplete. It's all a part of the whole.

ii

I don't know about too many people.
I mean, I don't think there's really too many.
Except in the cities.
But this means people have to move around more.
Like me.
My little island of a country (even if it *was* surrounded by land)— it just wasn't right for me.
I didn't like going places and being asked, "Do you know so-and-so?"
I needed more Lebensraum.
And here I am.

iii

I don't know about too many people.
Seems that the interesting people, people who might make good parents, just don't have children.

I'd like to have children, because I'd like to see them grow from the start.

But for God's sakes, not with just anyone.

iv

That's why I'm not gay.

I've tried it. I like it. I can get off on it.

And I have fun with it all, and I like a lot of the people I meet.

But why risk having your children taken away from you? By some bitter ex?

Better keep it simple. An occasional event maybe, gay or straight, but basically simple.

Kids.

Simple.

v

I am Martin.

Martin has no fancy duds.

Martin doesn't own a necktie.

Martin wants no fancy jobs.

Martin's hair is shampooed twice a week.

His teeth are brushed at least twice a day.

He has four shirts, three slacks, some socks and no underpants.

Two pairs of slacks are identical.

Oh yes, a pair of boots.

And a purple sweater.

Martin has some books— heck, no guitar.

And a casette tape recorder, that he has.

A car and a sense of humor.

He likes it simple and he likes to swim.

I am he, and he is Martin.

vi

    I'd rather just live alone.
    Or with someone with a light touch.
    A really and truly long thing— I don't think I'm ready for that. No, a light relationship is enough.
    Intense maybe, but only within the bounds.
    But nothing that would have to last a million years.
    A woman. And a kid.
    I think it has to be mine. Not sure.
    But simple, simple.
    Keep it simple.
    A house, some land. *My* job to keep it up, to pay for it. *My* job, to keep it warm and happy.
    Her job? The same as mine, I guess.

vii

    My hair is very long.
    That's years out of style now.
    I'm not to be trusted, according to the Man.
    It's as simple as that.
    Especially they figure I must do something too much. Sex or juice or grass. Actually I don't. Too much work to do.

viii

    Animals I like.
    Hiking I like.
    My car I like.
    Fuss I don't like,— or not being able to feel things.
    Not the greatest car, but I can fix everything that goes wrong with it.
    I like it simple.

ix

Bread. Money.
I guess I've got champagne tastes.
I do like good things.
And I don't like to pay for them.
But I also don't like waste.
So I don't like to waste my life and time unless I must.
No, I don't like waste.

x

God I don't know about.
But I'm sure he's on the same team as me.
Woods. Forests. Mountains. All those animals.
A little lake with wood chips floating in it.
The feel of someone's fanny in the morning.
There's an awful lot in the world.
    And I believe too much in things that weren't organized to think the world wasn't organized either— or maybe, ha ha, specially disorganized for the occasion.
    Arranged maybe.
    Anyway, words aren't my thing much. Call it what you want if you must call.

xi

My lady's left me.
I don't understand why.
We weren't just lovers. We were friends.
Really, she was my only friend.
Perhaps she wasn't ready for me. Maybe she'll
   never be.
But I'm pretty desolate, I guess.
Why did she do it to me?
She doesn't seem any happier with the guy she's with.

If she were, I could understand.
But for now, I don't.
It will be a long time before I'm ready for a scene like that again. If ever.
There's others who might love me, I guess.
But going through the motions of making love with them is like cold scrambled eggs. Or stale fried clams.
Kind of a travesty.
Let them love me, let them want me.
I'd rather jerk off.
But why did she do it to me?

xii

That's the trouble too with communes.
I'm sick of that scene too.
Everybody spends all their time talking about who's going to sleep with whom.
I don't like that.
One morning I woke up, and somebody was doing me. It felt good, but it bothered me. So I pretended to be asleep. And never once opened my eyes.
I have a pretty good idea who it was. But I could care less. Some people are dull.
Also, the smart ones wind up doing all the work.
And you never get a chance to make your own mistakes without everybody jumping on you.
The communes I *really* don't like are the ones where everything is everybody else's. Too confusing, and nothing gets done. When everything belongs to nobody, nobody wins.
I guess I could take the ones where a bunch of people just live together coöperatively, especially for some specific purpose.
But mostly I guess I've just gone through that all.

xiii

I am my own best company.
I like animals.
But I don't want a pet.
I wouldn't want an animal to depend on me.
After all, I can't depend on myself anymore.

xiv

What's it mean to learn?
I learn exactly what I need to learn, no more and no less.
Ambition for my work, dreams— these are things I have outgrown in the ordinary sense.
I dream that tomorrow, even if I can't be happy, I might be satisfied.
But these are people dreams, not mechanical ones, that go through my head. I could never be a doctor, like, because learning to be one would get in the way of my work.
Time is not my game or my commodity— it's just my home.
I cannot spend it, any more than you can spend *your* house.
There is nothing you can teach me which I can learn.

xv

I'll always be young.
I am Gulliver in Lilliput.
I am comfortable among mountains and big trees.
Not among rabbits and mice.
Plants, yes— they are a universe.
Dogs and bears have a function.
But flies are not my thing.
Mist is wonderful— it makes things big.

I like the softness of colors.

When I go away, it must be into softness and coolness. No edges.

Perhaps to disappear— a little man into a big sky.

Gently, yes, I understand gently.

Snow? I understand how snow must feel.

Sometimes I wish I gave a damn, though.

Barton, Vermont
December 2, 1973

for kathy k——

and he did,
and it's there,
after what they did,
and he said
from what she said
that he would,
but would she?
what they had,
hers and his,
did it.
and she knew
what they did
would do it.

milwaukee
11 february, 1977

selling futures on art works

    art
de art
depart
   p

                      new york
                      may 22, 1976

friend, what's going on here?

. . . . !
. . . . !
. . . . !
. . . . !
. . . . !
. . . . !
. . . . !
. . . . !
. . . . !
. . . . . . !
. . . . . !
. . . . !
. . . !
. . !
. !
!

!
! !
! ! !
! ! ! !
! ! ! ! !

milwaukee
11.ii.77!

poem from or for bern porter

i may mention his name
i may describe him
i may edit him
i may remove whole letter sections
i may do any or all above as i wish

i may indeed

                                          west glover
                                        30. vii. 76

lusus in
lose us in
lusus in
lose us in
lusus in
lose us in
lusus in
lose us in
lusus in
lose us in
lusus in
lose us in
lusus in
lose us in
lusus in
lose us in
lusus in
lose us in
lusus in
lose us in
lusus in
lose us in
lusus in
lose us in
lusus in
lose us in
lusus in
lose us in
lusus in
lose us in
lusus in
lose us in
lusus in
lose us in
lusus in
lose us in
lusus in
lose us in
lusus in
lose us in
lusus in
lose us in
lusus in
lose us in

waltz macabre

(milwaukee,
13 february, 1977)

Life

What if
Well then

New York
20.ii.75

words are mirrors

whose meanings
leap their neighbors from?

> milwaukee
> 17.iii.77

conceptual forks

to reveal the fish
from within the log
which the wood wanted to become—

is it a vanity?

8. V. 76
nyc

a commentary by the poet on
"conceptual forks"

i

does the wood want to become log or fish?

ii

(see *ecclesiastes* i, 2)
is "it" revealing the fish?
or the fish? the log? or the wood?
or a matter of names? calling "making a fish" "revealing?"

iii

what happened when the creation took place?
what happens when the creation takes place?

iv

can wood want? can wood be wanting? if so, what?
when is a fork not a fork?

v

(quote from bengt af klintberg: "music lies between the
            water and the stone")
can the meaning of a poem be a poem?
must the poem lie in the words?

vi

how does conceptualizing imply categories?
do these relate to chomsky's "transforms?"
what part of an empty cup is the most useful one?
does this explain my title?

vii

how many transforms are in my text?
is there any which does not pun on another transform?
how many ways can these be diagrammed?
are these modular units the poem?
are there any illegal units here?

viii

(see plotinus, 5th *ennead*, 8th tractate, opening section)
is the idea of the fish in the wood?
is the form of the fish in the wood?
who put it there?
can ideas become forms? or forms ideas?
if they were fused, which would dominate?

ix

whose is the idea of the fish?
whose is the fish?
where, then, is the vanity?
can "vanity" imply being "in vain?"
can existence be in vain?
where does this place the poem?

nyc
11. V. 76

definition

    i'd rather   love you
but i'd rather not lose you

       let's get to work

                              barton, vermont
                              july 25, 1973

it could be you too

me in a big hat
me fat and sassy
me trying to start my car
me miserable in cold winds
me laughing with a mechanic
me with an icicled moustache

me playing scales on my typewriter
me working with an open door
me welcoming
me with a handful of fizz
me delighted by some sunshine
me enjoying the good view

me laughing with my nephew
me watching the buffalo shit
me feeling like a seal
me and vanilla ice cream
me stuffed like a doll

me walking through a hot day
me slicing the heavy sunlight
me delighted by a big basket
me censored

me enjoying the clean sand
me longing to shrink a bit
me considering lunchtime
me observing the water's wetness
me chilled
me just fine

me remembering my daughters
me lonely for someone special
me and a ridiculous telephone
me totally communicated at
me giggling at the wind

me in a serious conversation
me trying to be helpful
me all thumbs
me blushing with a friend

me my wife and my lover
me hither across the land
me and outrageous architecture
me and the nature of oak trees
me and a sudden mushroom
me around the maying

me and a moorish dome in the suburbs
me in the door of a church
me and the loveliest hymns
me and colored light squares on the pews
me informed i'm unhappy
me deeply thankful yes thankful

me and a friend and a stew
me and the first leaves on a street
me and the last snowpile of april
me and a soft shadow to walk after

me and the morning and evening of working
me and the twilight and biggest eyed cars
me and warm evenings and movies to go to
me cooking chinese but with the wrong soysauce
me around midnight contented to sleep

me and you and
stars and cars and
him and her and
him and him and
day and night and
work and play and
tears and help and
cold and hot and
clothed and nude and
one and two and
walked and run and
once and twice and
doors and rooms and
in and out and
talked and still and
fat and thin and
chopped and smoothed and
yes and no and
round and round and
yes!

good morning!

milwaukee
4 february, '77

HA
  A
  AH
 HA
  AH
  A

7/23/71

moving

not so clean
      of pictures
up and down
      of pictures
brightness

the big room
      a grand piano
      a grand piano
      two small tables
      a grand piano

should i
      rent out
      to a tenant?
can i
      stay?
can i
      move
      to my friend?
shall i
      stay?
should i
      stay?

the big room
      a big red rug
      two small tables
      lots of records
      two small tables

the big room
>	lots of records
>	with a couch
>	a grand piano
>	lots of records
>	a big red rug
>	lots of records
>	a big red rug
>	lots of records
>	two small tables

brightness
>	the staircase
up and down
>	the stairwell

counters
>	from summer's garden
and cupboards
>	from last year
and cupboards

dried foods
>	with treats
candy jars
>	from summer's garden
counters
>	a little messy

the big room
>	lots of records
>	and books

frozen foods
>	gathered in summer

to tack down

counters
      for working on
frozen foods
      from summer's garden
and cupboards
      from summer's garden
counters
      from last year

the big room
      and books
      and books

mysterious bags
      from last year
mysterious bags
      with treats

can i
      give up
      my music?

to tack down
      each step rug
variety
      the staircase
up and down
      the walls
up and down
      the stairwell
to tack down
      the stairwell

counters
> a little messy
and cupboards
> with treats
counters
> from summer gardens
variety
> each step rug
not so clean
> the staircase

to tack down
> the staircase
variety
> of pictures
needing painting
> the walls
to tack down
> the stairwell
up and down
> the staircase
up and down
> the staircase
not so clean
> each step rug
not so clean
> of pictures
up and down
> the walls
brightness
> the stairwell

toasting
> watching the coals

stars
    watching the coals
where we sit
    in winter

the big room
    and books

to tack down
    the stairwell
needing painting
    of pictures

brightness
    the walls
not so clean
    each step rug
up and down
    of pictures
up and down
    each step rug

king size bed
    more interesting than pretty
view of barton mountain
    more interesting than pretty
table i had
    witness to much loving
view of barton mountain
    we lay and watched
table i had

                            barton, vermont
                            june 4, 1975

fight

1) a room stripped bare except for:

2) soft objects of all kinds— pillows, stuffed toy animals, feathers, green leaves, snow, etc.

3) visitors violently throwing these things at each other, clobbering each other with them.

4) nobody hurt.

barton, vermont
september, 1972

28 things to think about, a manifesto

1) my hair   is my hair   and corresponds to nothing.
2) " ear   " " ear   " "   " " .
3) " face   " " face   " "   " " .
4) " eye   " " eye   " "   " " .
5) " brow   " " brow   " "   " " .
6) " nose   " " nose   " "   " " .
7) " lip   " " lip   " "   " " .
8) " tooth   " " tooth   " "   " " .
9) " chin   " " chin   " "   " " .
10)" neck   " " neck   " "   " " .
11)" shoulder" " shoulder" "   " " .
12)" arm   " " arm   " "   " " .
13)" elbow   " " elbow   " "   " " .
14)" wrist   " " wrist   " "   " " .
15)" hand   " " hand   " "   " " .
16)" palm   " " palm   " "   " " .
17)" finger   " " finger   " "   " " .
18)" chest   " " chest   " "   " " .
19)" belly   " " belly   " "   " " .
20)" hip   " " hip   " "   " " .
21)" cock   " " cock   " "   " " .
22)" ball   " " ball   " "   " " .
23)" thigh   " " thigh   " "   " " .
24)" knee   " " knee   " "   " " .
25)" shin   " " shin   " "   " " .
26)" ankle   " " ankle   " "   " " .
27)" foot   " " foot   " "   " " .
28)" toe   " " toe   " "   " " .

§§§§§§§§§§§§§§§§§§§§§§§§§§§§

p. s.---

" " "   " " "   " "   " "   "

                             nyc
                             30.x.75

song

is round six
is round earth
is round of boxers
is round

is round fat
is round big
is round sung
is round

is round midnight
is round my room
is round beef
is round

barton, vermont
june 4, 1975

portrait of a woman

                she is
                she is alive
     warm she is
                she is angry
    round she is
                she is anxious
    ready she is
                she is broke
   lonely she is
                she is caring
interested she is
                she is difficult
   gentle she is
                she is

                                  new canaan, ct
                                  17. ii. 75

leather jacket vaudeville

cat under arm. tail in mouth.
squeeze. bite.
bagpipes.

barton, vermont
may 28th, 1972

to my brother and sister english teachers

    why
    asked for bread
    must we give the same old stones?

milwaukee
2 april '77

old man

the bigness of cities
the silence of children
the slowness of dying

berlin
18 october, 1973

memories of the 1950's

mashed sandwiches
heterosexuals at a waterfall
wintercress and sour cream

bvm
30.ix.74

to whom it may concern:

do you remember the first dada object?
did eve give it to adam?
or will you give it to me?

7 april, 1976
new york, ny

deep summer together poem

for g

i – brook

long
water

together

                                                 silver

rocks   at the *edges*

games   *black*

                                        at the *depths*

bubbles
floating
boats

evening   deep   summertime

sound   to wade   lifetime

morning   deep

how *long*

how *water*

together

ii – smokes

afterward   green

together   day

books   sitting

in bed   gravel

books

together

  pale   no
  pernod   seed
  yellow   no

         rising
         crescent
         soft
         outcurve

  blow   colombia
  through   mexico
  tube   vermont

         silent   hunger
         voice   ice cream
         silent   hunger

         eyes   strong
         meet   held in

  puff
  fondle
  high
  puff

         together

         iii – clouds

  sky   blue
  face   white
  sky   blue

                anvils
                over hills

  round bottom   part *this* way
  sharp top   part *that* way

         together

flow
large
flow

this   move
that   move
this

maybe a *storm*
maybe a *shine*

                    mending   clouds
                    clouds   eating
                    mending   clouds

                    blue
                    drifting

mist
learning to be
cloud

                    being
                    clouds
                    together

                    iv – nights

hand
    over *stomach*   the cat
mind   with
    over *matter*   the dog

                    together

half closed   base of skull
eyes   shoulders
half closed   triangle

                                  touching   white
                                  lipping   flower
                                  favoring   oil

long hair
on my chest

hardness
to my fingers
of the ass

                                  butterfly   playing hammer
                                  touch   dulcimer back

                                                           cocooned
                                                           alone
                                                           over there

                                suddenly
                                here
                                sleeping

                                touch
                                boob
                                tube
                                up

rounded   crescent   to go
hollow   below   half spent

                                                           to bring
                                                           to melt

                                gnash   cool
                                teeth   nipple
                                sleep   cool

                                together

                        v – trees

shivering
like teeth
in the cold

                        together

cut   spruce
shape   cedar
cut   hemlock

cedar
sunbathing

                        saw   captain kidd
                        chain   treasure
                        saw   here

undressing   trees
trees   revealing
                                        trees

                        balsam

teeth   shivering
sharpening   before the fall
yes   shivering

                        together

                        vi – small talk

know   wee
you'd   shall
rather not   see

                                        who
                                        knows
                                        but doesn't say

```
                    to
summertime          knot
     lifetime       to

                    together

not                 it's              a long time
into                heavy             a long day
that

now                 yes
not                 yes
now

                    okay              not
                    together          rather
                    okay              not

as well             sure
might               okay
as well             sure


                                      not forever
                                      but now

                    cool

not
too long
not

                    together

                                      bvm
                                      13.7.74
```

Something Borrowed

A woman's face with Nature's own hand painted
Hast thou, the master mistress of my passion;
A woman's gentle heart but not acquainted
With shifting change as is false women's fashion;
An eye more bright than theirs, less false in rolling,
Gilding the object whereupon it gazeth;
A man in hue all hues in his controlling,
Which steals men's eyes and women's souls amazeth.
And for a woman wert thou first created,
Till Nature as she wrought thee fell a-doting,
And by addition thee of me defeated,
By adding one thing to my purpose nothing.
      But since she prick'd thee out for women's pleasure,
      Mine be thy love, and thy love's use their treasure.

January 7, 1974
New York City

Sonnet: "Of Barton winds my breath is made"

Of Barton winds my breath is made; my thoughts
        Are eggs, hatched out to plain air by the sun.
That clear sky clarifies my shoulds and oughts,
        For there the mind's whirl stops when day is done.

Among dark canyons and concrete towers I'm pressed,
        Raced faceless to myself, alone in crowds,
Seeing close friends but rarely, trussed and dressed
        And cannibalized, my feelings disguised by shrouds.

The cream of the Jest is lost here, Its sense fled;
        When icebox faces must be treated with respect
Each day turns mere transition from bed to bed,
        And I wonder, will I ever be free to elect

To slosh across grey hayfields once again,
        Foolish and shivering in October rain?

                                New York
                                26 September, 1976

abstand zum abstand veb

i

gnawz
gnawznegeg
gnawznegegrev vergegenzwang
                gegenzwang
gnawz   zwang
gnawznegeg
gnawznegegrev vergegenzwang
                gegenzwang
gnawz   zwang
gnawznegeg
gnawznegegrev vergegenzwang
                gegenzwang
gnawz   zwang
gnawznegeg
gnawznegegrev vergegenzwang
                gegenzwang
gnawz   zwang
gnawznegeg
gnawznegegrev vergegenzwang
                gegenzwang
gnawz   zwang
gnawznegeg
gnawznegegrev vergegenzwang
                gegenzwang
                        zwang

ii

vergegenständlichmachung   vergegenständlichung
  gegenständlichmachung zur   gegenständlichung
     ständlichmachung zur   ständlichung
           machung zur   ung
                  zur

iii

zur god incorporate

                new york, usa, veb
                20. oktober, 1976

this word

symbolizes symbol:
    symbol

                              milwaukee, wisconsin
                                    april 2nd, 1977

3 reflections on poststructuralism

i

of what are you a symbol?

ii

do you see yourself
    seeing yourself?

is that how you see?

iii (ref. blake)

the trick is to see ourselves
through our eyes and
through our minds

not just with them

denver
4.v.77

lyronic: no birding permitted

dark black those green mountains
maying them together
           with an evening hand
                  unstopping
                      unceasable

no birds yes
yes birds no

good kiss
sweet night

                                      denver
                                      4.v.77

love song for straights

push her valves
pull her buttons
decorate her corners
moisten her edges
and squeeze her accordion

wind up his springs
lick his eyelids heavy
touch up his garden path
toy with his cauliflower
and squeeze his accordion

walk along your bridge of sighs
drum along your shoulder
investigate your nostril
contemplate your rib cage
and squeeze your accordion

yes to my frozen angles
yes to this elbow here
yes to my lifting plains
yes to my hidden streams
but squeeze my accordion

milwaukee
23rd march, 1977

Put Differently, Another Socratic Question
           for Mike Belt

?

Mind changed,
What do you do
      do you do with the rejected
                            idea
      do you do with the rejected
What do you do
Mind changed,

?

                                        Milwaukee
                                        18 March, 1977

You're in the News Today
– a proposed environment –

1) A medium sized room—2000 square feet—the walls and backs of doors entirely covered with mirror surfaces (or ferrotype plates, or mirror vinyl, etc.). Floors and ceilings matte black.

2) A movie projector showing the most recent news films that can be obtained.

3) A carousel slide projector showing war photographs or atrocities.

4) Another carousel projector showing black-and-white slide footage of very recent newspapers.

5) An opaque projector showing the newspaper of the day the environment is experienced.

6) Some recent newspapers crumpled on the floor.

7) A radio playing only newscasts. Optional: several such radios, but tuned to different stations.

8) Two more optionals: *a*, a number of recent headlines silkscreened in white matte or "sandblast effect" ink onto some of the mirrors. And *b*, some retractable screens or areas to project on if they do not get in the way.

9) Audience comes in one door, and goes out the other, never more than three or four people inside at a time.

Barton, Vermont
February-December, 1972

two insincerities
for m.c.

i

i could speak with you
    about my house in the snow
    about my fondness for old wood
    about my daughters' eyes
    about how i met their mother
    about my favorite clouds
or should i speak with you about what's on my mind?

i could speak with you
    about your sister's girlfriend
    about your stepbrother's wedding
    about your practicing problem
    about the words that you don't like
    about the things that you aren't doing
or should i speak to you about what's on my mind?

i could speak with you
    about his history
    about the things that he invented
    about bad things he did to people
    about funny things that happened to him
    about the way his ears could wiggle
or should i speak to you about what's on my mind?

i could speak with you
    about her skinny laughter
    about feeling with her feet as she climbed a ladder
    about the things she'd meant to do
    about dancing with her at the peppermint lounge
    about the mess she was in when last i saw her
or should i speak to you about what's on my mind?

 i could speak with you
    about the lessons of turkish history
    about the need to smash all nationalisms
    about net surplus value
    about the nitrogen cycle and algae
    about the ways wild mushrooms grow
or should i speak to you about what's on my mind?

i could speak with you
    about wanting to run with you
    about woods things that we might do together
    about platforms we could build together
    about our bonfires and performances
    about places we might go together like sweden
or should i speak to you about what's on my mind?

i could speak with you
    about their concerts and their markets
    about how they make white hors-d'oeuvres of
     people
    about their clams and their funiculars
    about the history of their leaders' thoughts
    about their 1700 brands of ski wax
or shall i speak to you about what's on my mind?

ii

come to me when you need laughter
i'll try to help you laugh, guffaw with you

come to me when you need to yell at someone
i won't be yelling back, but i'll be glad you came

come to me with rancour on your lips
i'll drink with you, and blow the glum away

come to me when you need lying to
i'll never lie, but help to lift the veils

come to me when work is to be done
i'll work with you, since that's what it's about

come to me if ever you need love
i won't believe you, but i'll give it to you

come to me if you need to be welcome
you're welcome

barton, vermont
november 22, 1971

Appearances and Disappearance
– for Pauline Oliveros –

Hair becomes— becomes its wearer and becomes grey. Grey as this. Time's passing. Or that.

Toast it? No, please don't. We can celebrate it without toasting it. I drink no alcohol: a toast in water does not float deeply in the mind. But if we toast it, let it be in sunshine. Sunshine becoming— becoming to her, even when she shuts her eyes. Becoming twilight. Becoming twilight to her. To her. Earlier, becoming red. Setting.

The setting of hair.

Shutting her eyes, squinting.

A pool. Yes, a pool, no a pool but yes a pool. Not mere appearance when you get wet from it, no? Quite a pool and quiet a pool. Much talk of music, listing to pipe's vibration as electronic flute. "A hive of bees," she said. And it was, but it wasn't: an appearance.§ A flute without a flute, a bee without a bee. Being without being. Being without clothes, those appearances of whom one is not. And in a pool. Cool. But no, not particularly cold. Yes and no— moving in the same direction. Particularly wet. Perhaps particularly nice.

Quiet that day. This day and that day, this and that. Say, was it only yesterday? Did you say it? What did I say? What shall I say? Say say? No, that'll be a lark. This and that'll be a lark, one day. Larks say so much, anyday, here in Vermont. Someday, anyday— mayday!

Rather quietly, that day, seeming to be quiet. Appearance, without worrying about appearance. Quite naked, quiet wet, a quiet wet of sound. Noisy on another but now seeming,

§ No, I don't believe Satie's stage directions in his music— they appear and they evoke appearance. The notes lie within the notes, and the directions within the directions. If he suggests "sans sécheresse" try a little "sécheresse."

that day. To be alone among us, when one's head is slightly under and more than slightly wet— a day of sun and hair in the water becoming grey. Grey sun, grey hair, grey water. Like the beaming of hair, the streaming of air— beaming into one's eyes.

We are not beautiful but we are beautiful: is it misappearance? I do like to have a lark. I know you do, you too. For a lark we went to Wheeler Mountain: no grey that day. Raspberries and blueberries. Algonkin word for a heaven: a place with many berries in it. Blueberries on a blue day. Wind? To wind up a wind, but not release it. Taught and taut. Still it was windless.

Long ago they wheeled her mountain, Wheeler Mountain. And where the dirt fell off the berries grew. And the rocks stayed bare where the dirt had disappeared: big but gentle cliffs and crags, with sunshine in their eyes like yours.

Up the hill— not big but broad, like you. I like you. Dark woods: would there were mushrooms. And there were mushrooms (hiding in the woods like night, keeping watch over there). Mysterious appearances where one had been looking. Finding us. Lightly finding us, light and not burning. Beaming into hemlock. Spruce, spruced up.

Open space. Hers and his story: how the house was built. And how we got here. Over this hill. And that. Towards New Hampshire and away from it. From what. From it. It all. All of it, little it— belittle it down a ravine and up. Open a space and pour out rock. A beam of rock without a beam of light: a beam's appearance or disappearance. Shadows talking talk but little. Opened a top. Atop Wheeler Mountain. Stop. Sit a little.

Shadows fattening. Eating the silence. Up— out and down, following the mind's hand. A tractor in a field, one sound. Two. Many. Too many trees to count. Hillfuls, dalefuls. How hillful that dale and there a lake. Grey lake of blue: earth's eye. I sat, we sat— another woman, a dog too. Four for a moment, for four a moment. Another hidden sound: she said she didn't hear it. An appearance with a disappearance behind it. Cows: there not here. Theirs not ours. Clear days and thours— the clear behind the clear. And blue. And passing. And passing blue behind all blue.

Grey blue of lake. Earth's eye is ours.

And blue. And passing. And passing shadow behind all shadow. And blue. And shadow. And grey. And shadow. And days and hours are ours, behind days and hours of hours.

Wheeler Mountain: disappearance and appearance.§

A leapdog and a shadow.

It's going time.

Disappearances including appearances. Really and truly being there. Pleasing to appear often. Down a mountain. Or in other ways. On other days.

Barton, Vermont
25 July, 1976

§ . . . Of rare and romantic beauty, and which looks like an engraving.

Other books by Dick Higgins include

What Are Legends (1960)
Jefferson's Birthday/Postface (1964)
Towards the 1970's (1969)
FOEW&OMBWHNW (1969)
Die Fabelhafte Geträume von Taifun-Willi (1970)
Computers for the Arts (1970)
amigo (1972)
A Book About Love & War & Death (1972)
The Ladder to the Moon (1973)
For Eugene in Germany (1973)
Gesehen, Gehört und Verstanden (1973)
Le Petit Cirque au Fin du Monde (1973)
Spring Game (1973)
City With All the Angles (1974)
Modular Poems (1975)
Legends & Fishnets (1976)
classic plays (1976)
Cat Alley (1976)
George Herbert's Pattern Poems: In Their Tradition (1977)
Vintage Higgins (forthcoming)

Edited by Dick Higgins and Wolf Vostell

Fantastic Architecture (1971)

750 copies of *everyone has sher favorite* (*his or hers*) have been printed, of which 50 copies were bound in cloth, signed and numbered.

this book was set in monotype bell, a typeface designed by richard austin in 1788 for john bell, a printer and publisher in london, england. the paper is warren's olde style. typesetting, printing and binding were done by the stinehour press of lunenburg, vermont, in october, 1977